MW00872731

Funny Jokes

Ultimate LOL
Edition

Copyright Notice

General Disclaimer

A young boy asks his Dad, "What is the difference between confident and confidential?
Dad says, "You are my son, I'm confident about that. Your friend over there, is also my son, that's confidential! "

Husband: "When I get mad at you, you never fight back. How do you control your anger?"
Wife: "I clean the toilet."
Husband: "How does that help?"
Wife: "I use your toothbrush."

Son: Mum, when I was on the bus with Dad this morning, he told me to give up my seat to a lady!
Mum: Well, you have done the right thing.
Son: But mum, I was sitting on dad's lap.

A woman decides to have a facelift for her 50th birthday. She spends $15,000 and feels pretty good about the results. On her way home, she stops at a news stand to buy a newspaper. Before leaving, she says to the clerk,

"I hope you don't mind my asking, but how old do you think I am?"

"About 32," is the reply.

"Nope! I'm exactly 50," the woman says happily.

A little while later she goes into McDonald's and asks the counter girl the very same question. The girl replies,

"I'd guess about 29."

The woman replies with a big smile,

"Nope, I'm 50."

Now she's feeling really good about herself. She stops in a drug store on her way down the street. She goes up to the counter to get some mints and asks the clerk this burning question. The clerk responds,

"Oh, I'd say 30."

Again she proudly responds,

"I'm 50, but thank you!"

While waiting for the bus to go home, she asks an old man waiting next to her the same question. He replies,

"I'm 78 and my eyesight is going. Although, when I was young, there was a sure-fire way to tell how old a woman was. If you permit me to put my hands under your bra, then, and only then can I tell you EXACTLY how old you are."

They wait in silence on the empty street until her curiosity gets the best of her.

She finally blurts out,

"What the hell, go ahead."

He slips both of his hands under her blouse and begins to feel around very slowly and carefully. He bounces and weighs each breast and he gently pinches each nipple. He pushes her breasts together and rubs them against each other.

After a couple of minutes of this, she says,

"Okay, okay...How old am I?"

He completes one last squeeze of her breasts, removes his hands, and says " Ma dam, you are 50."

Stunned and amazed, the woman says,

"That was incredible, how could you tell?"

The old man says,

"Promise you won't get mad?"

"I promise I won't," she says.

"I was behind you in McDonald's."

The General went out to find that none of his G.I.s were there. One finally ran up, panting heavily.

"Sorry, sir! I can explain, you see I had a date and it ran a little late. I ran to the bus but missed it, I hailed a cab but it broke down, found a farm, bought a horse but it dropped dead, ran 10 miles, and now I'm here."

The General was very skeptical about this explanation but at least he was here so he let the G.I. go. Moments later, eight more G.I.s came up to the general panting, he asked them why they were late.

"Sorry, sir! I had a date and it ran a little late, I ran to the bus but missed it, I hailed a cab but it broke down, found a farm, bought a horse but it dropped dead, ran 10 miles, and now I'm here."

The General eyed them, feeling very skeptical but since he let the first guy go, he let them go, too. A ninth G.I. jogged up to the General, panting heavily.

"Sorry, sir! I had a date and it ran a little late, I ran to the bus but missed it, I hailed a cab but..."

"Let me guess," the General interrupted, "it broke down."

"No," said the G.I., "there were so many dead horses in the road, it took forever to get around them."

Airman Jones was assigned to the induction center where he was to advise new recruits about their government benefits, especially their GI insurance.

It wasn't long before Captain Smith noticed that Airman Jones had almost a 100% record for insurance sales, which had never happened before.

Rather than ask about this, the Captain stood in the back of the room and listened to Jones's sales pitch. Jones explained the basics of the GI Insurance to the new recruits, and then said:

"If you have GI Insurance and go into battle and are killed, the government has to pay $200,000 to your beneficiaries. If you don't have GI insurance, and you go into battle and get killed, the government has to pay only a maximum of $6000."

"Now," he concluded, "Which bunch do you think they are going to send into battle first?"

After working most of her life Grandma finally retired. At her next checkup, the new doctor told her to bring a list of all the medicines that had been prescribed for her.

As the young doctor was looking through these, his eyes grew wide as he realized she had a prescription for birth control pills.

"Mrs. Smith, do you realize these are BIRTH CONTROL pills?"

"Yes, they help me sleep at night."

"Mrs. Smith, I assure you there is absolutely NOTHING in these that could possibly help you sleep!

She reached out and patted the young Doctor's knee. "Yes, dear, I know that. But every morning, I grind one up and mix it in the glass of orange juice that my 16 year old granddaughter drinks . . . and believe me, it helps me sleep at night. "

An old man was eating in a truck stop when three bikers walked in.

The first walked up to the old man, pushed his cigarette into the old man's pie and then took a seat at the counter.

The second walked up to the old man, spit into the old man's milk and then he took a seat at the counter.

The third walked up to the old man, turned over the old man's plate, and then he took a seat at the counter.

Without a word of protest, the old man quietly left the diner.

Shortly thereafter, one of the bikers said to the waitress, "Humph, not much of a man, was he?"

The waitress replied, "Not much of a truck driver either. He just backed his truck over three motorcycles."

A little boy got on the bus, sat next to a man reading a book, and noticed he had his collar on backwards. The little boy asked why he wore his collar that way.

The man, who was a priest, said, "I am a Father"

The little boy replied, "My Daddy doesn't wear his collar like that".

The priest looked up from his book and answered, "I am the Father of many".

The boy said, "My Dad has 4 boys, 4 girls and two grandchildren and he doesn't wear his collar that way".

The priest, getting impatient, said, "I am the Father of hundreds" and went back to reading his book.

The little boy sat quietly thinking for a while, then leaned over and said, "Maybe you should wear your pants backwards instead of your collar".

It was George the Mailman's last day on the job after 35 years of carrying the mail through all kinds of weather to the same neighborhood.

When he arrived at the first house on his route, he was greeted by the whole family who congratulated him and sent him on his way with a tidy gift envelope.

At the second house, they presented him with a box of fine cigars.

The folks at the third house handed him a selection of terrific fishing lures.

At the fourth house, he was met at the door by a strikingly beautiful blonde woman in a revealing negligee. She took him by the hand, gently led him through the door, which she closed behind him, and took him up the stairs to the bedroom where she blew his mind with the most passionate love he had ever experienced.

When he had enough, they went downstairs and she fixed him a giant breakfast: eggs, potatoes, ham, sausage, blueberry waffles, and fresh-squeezed orange juice.

When he was truly satisfied, she poured him a cup of steaming coffee. As she was pouring, he noticed a dollar bill sticking out from under the cup's bottom edge.

"All this was just too wonderful for words," he said, "But what's the dollar for?"

"Well," she said. "Last night, I told my husband that today would be your last day, and that we should do something special for you. I asked him what to give you.

He said, "Screw him. Give him a dollar." The breakfast was my idea."

Blind Date

A guy gets set up on a blind date and he takes her out for dinner to a very expensive restaurant to make a good impression. The waiter approaches the table and asks to take their order.

The lady begins ordering practically everything on the menu, shrimp cocktail, pate, Caesar Salad, lobster, crepes Suzette, with no regard to the price. The guy is getting very upset, as he never thought she would order so much.

She then stops, and looks across at him, and asks,

"What do you suggest I wash it down with?"

"Well my dear, I can think of nothing so fitting as the Mississippi River."

By the time John pulled into the little town, every hotel room was taken.

"You've got to have a room somewhere." he pleaded to the last hotel manager. "Or just a bed--I don't really care where. I'm completely exhausted"

"Well, I do have a double room with one occupant," admitted the manager, "and I'm sure he would be glad to split the cost. But to tell you the truth, he snores so loudly that people in adjoining rooms have complained all week. I'm not sure it'd be worth it to you."

"No problem," the tired traveler assured him. "I'll take it."

The next morning John came down to breakfast bright-eyed and bushy-tailed. The manager asked him how he survived.

"Never better." John said.

The manager was impressed. "No problem with the other guy snoring, then?"

"Nope. I shut him up in no time."

"How'd you manage that?"

"He was already in bed, snoring away, when I came in the room." John said. "I went over, gave him a kiss on the cheek, said, "Good night, beautiful" and he sat up all night watching me."

Fred gets married and on his wedding night he calls his Father for some tips on what to do, since he has never been with a woman before.

"So what do I do first?"?

His father replied, "Take her clothes off and lay her on the bed."

5 minutes later Fred's on the phone again.

"She's naked and in bed, what do I do now???

His father can't believe what he is hearing, "Take your damn clothes off and get into bed with her."

After another 5 minutes poor Fred is on the phone again.

"Dad, I'm naked and in bed with her, what do I do now?"

His dad's patience is now running thin so he says, "Shit son! Do I have to spell everything out for you? Just put the hardest thing on your body where she pees. Goodnight!!!"

Just when the old man starts snoring, his son is on the phone once again.
"Ok Dad, I have my head in the toilet bowl what do I do next"

"DROWN YOURSELF, YOU F**KING IDIOT!!

After being married for thirty years, a wife asked her husband to describe her.

He looked at her for a while ... then said, "You're A, B, C, D, E, F, G, H, I, J, K."

She asks ... "What does that mean?"

He said, "Adorable, Beautiful, Cute, Delightful, Elegant, Foxy, Gorgeous, and Hot".

She smiled happily and said ... "Oh, that's so lovely ... What about I, J, K?"

He said, "I'm Just Kidding"

Knife Juggler, driving to his next performance, was stopped by the police. "What are those knives doing in your car?" asked the officer.
"I juggle them in my act."
"Oh yeah?" says the cop. "Let's see you do it."

So the juggler starts tossing and juggling the knives. A guy driving by sees this and says, "Wow, am I glad I quit drinking. Look at the test they're making you do now!"

An attorney telephoned the governor just after midnight, insisting that he talk to him regarding a matter of utmost urgency. An aide eventually agreed to wake up the governor.

"So, what is it?", grumbled the governor.

"Judge Garber has just died", said the attorney, and I want to take his place.

Replied the governor: "Well, it's OK with me if it's OK with the undertaker".

Married 25 years, I took a look at my wife one day and said, "Honey, 25 years ago, we had a cheap apartment, a cheap car, slept on a sofa bed and watched a 10 inch black and white TV, but I got to sleep every night with a hot 25 year old blonde.

Now, we have a nice house, nice car, big bed and plasma screen TV, but I'm sleeping with a 50 year old woman. It seems to me that you are not holding up your side of things."

My wife is a very reasonable woman. She told me to go out and find a hot 25 year old blonde, and she would make sure that I would once again be living in a cheap apartment, driving a cheap car, sleeping on a sofa bed.

Jon and Matt have been promoted from privates to sergeants.

Not long after, they're out for a walk and Jon says, "Hey, Matt, there's the Officers Club. Let's you and me stop in."

"But were privates," protests Matt.

"Were sergeants now," says Jon, pulling him inside.

"Now, Matt, I'm gonna sit down and have me a drink."

"But were privates," says Matt.

"You blind?" asks Jon, pointing at his stripes. "Were sergeants are now."

So they have their drink, and pretty soon a hooker comes up to Jon. "You'r cute," she says, "and I'd like to screw you, but I've got a bad case of gonorrhea."

Jon pulls his friend to the side and whispers, "Matt, go look in the dictionary and see what "gonorrhea" means. If it's okay, give me the okay sign."

So Matt goes to look it up, comes back, and gives Jon the big okay sign.

Three weeks later Jon is laid up in the infirmary with a terrible case of gonorrhea.

"Matt," he says, "Why'd you give me the okay?"

"Well, Jon, in the dictionary, it say gonorrhea affects only the privates."

He points to his stripes. "But were sergeants now."

MY IDEA OF CONFUSION!!

Two men met at a bus stop and struck up a conversation. One of them kept complaining of family problems. Finally, the other man said:

"You think you have family problems? Listen to my situation. A few years ago I met a young widow with a grown-up daughter and we got married". "Later my father married my step daughter. That made my step daughter my stepmother and my father became my stepson. Also, my wife became mother in-law of her father-in-law. Then the daughter of my wife, my stepmother, had a son. This boy was my half-brother because he was my father's son, but he was also the son of my wife's daughter which made him my wife's grand-son. That made me the grandfather of my half-brother.

"This was nothing until my wife and I had a son. Now the half-sister of my son, my stepmother, is also the grandmother. "This makes my father the brother-in-law of my child, whose stepsister is my father's wife, I'm my stepmother's brother-in-law, my wife is her own child's aunt, my son is my father's nephew and I'm my own grandfather!

A man and his wife were awakened at 3:00 am by a loud pounding on the door.

The man gets up and goes to the door where a drunken stranger, standing in the pouring rain, is asking for a push.

"Not a chance," says the husband, "it is 3:00 in the morning!"

He slams the door and returns to bed.

"Who was that?" asked his wife.

"Just some drunk guy asking for a push," he answers.

"Did you help him?" she asks.

"No, I did not, it's 3am in the morning and it's well pouring with rain out there!"

"Well, you have a short memory," says his wife. "Can't you remember about three months ago when we broke down, and those two guys helped us? I think you should help him, and you should be ashamed of yourself! "God loves drunk people too you know."

The man does as he is told, gets dressed, and goes out into the pounding rain.

He calls out into the dark, "Hello, are you still there?"

"Yes," comes back the answer.

"Do you still need a push?" calls out the husband.

"Yes, please!" comes the reply from the dark.

"Where are you?" asks the husband.

"Over here on the swing," replied the drunk.

Dentist to Patient: To extract your tooth will cost you $600!
Patient: What!! $600 for just a few minutes work?
Dentist: Well, I can extract it very slowly if you like.

At Heathrow airport in England, a 300-foot red carpet was stretched out to Air Force One and President Bush strode to a warm but dignified hand shake from Queen Elizabeth II. They rode in a silver 1934 Bentley to the edge of Central London where they boarded an open 17th century coach hitched to six magnificent white horses.

As they rode towards Buckingham Palace, each looking to their side and waving to thousands of cheering Britons lining the streets, all was going well. This was indeed a glorious display of pageantry and dignity. Suddenly the scene was shattered when the right rear horse let rip the most horrendous, earth-shattering, eye-smarting blast of flatulence, and the coach immediately filled with noxious fumes.

Uncomfortable, but maintaining control, the two dignitaries did their best to ignore the whole incident, but then the Queen decided that was a most ridiculous manner with which to handle a most embarrassing situation. She turned to Mr. Bush and explained, "Mr. President, please accept my regrets. I'm sure you understand that there are some things even a Queen cannot control."

George W., ever the Texas gentleman, replied, "Your Majesty, please don't give the matter another thought. You know, if you hadn't said something I would have assumed it was one of the horses."

A man and his ever-nagging wife went on vacation in Jerusalem. While they were there, the wife passed away. The undertaker told the husband, "You can have her buried here in the Holy Land for 1500 or we can have her shipped back home for 50000."

The husband thought about it and told the undertaker he would have her shipped back home. The undertaker asked him, "why would you spend 50000 to have her shipped home when you could have a beautiful burial here, and it would only cost 1500?"

The husband replied, "Long ago, a man (JESUS) died here, was buried here, and three days later, rose from the dead. I just can't take that chance!"

A lady went to the store to buy a parrot and asks the sales person, "how much is the parrot cost?" "twenty quid", says the sales person.

"What's so special about the parrot ?" she asks...

Sales person: "This parrot can talk",

So the lady asks the parrot, "how do I look?"

The parrot replies, "you look like a f*cking Slut?"

The lady gets pissed off and tells the sales person that it's a very rude parrot and she cannot buy it. The sales person tells her to please wait for 2 minutes.

The sales person takes the parrot to the back of the store and shoves the parrot into a bucket of water and when he pulls the parrot out he says, "if you disrespect the lady out there, I'll soak you in water again" and takes the parrot back outside.

The sales person asked the lady to ask the parrot another question.

Lady: "If I come home with 1 man what would you think?"

Parrot: "He's your husband"

Lady: "2 men",

Parrot: "Your husband and his brother",

Lady: "3 men",

Parrot: "Your husband, his brother & your brother"

Lady: "4 men",

Parrot: "Bring the f*cking bucket of water, I already told you she's a slut!"

In Florida, an atheist created a case against the upcoming Easter and Passover Holy days. He hired an attorney to bring a discrimination case against Christians and Jews and observances of their holy days. The argument was that it was unfair that atheists had no such recognized days.

The case was brought before a judge. After listening to the passionate presentation by the lawyer, the judge banged his gavel declaring, "Case dismissed!"

The lawyer immediately stood objecting to the ruling saying,

"Your honour, How can you possibly dismiss this case? The Christians have Christmas, Easter and others. The Jews have Passover, Yom Kippur and Hanukkah, yet my client and all other atheists have no such holidays."

The judge leaned forward in his chair saying, "But you do. Your client, counsel, is woefully ignorant."

The lawyer said, "Your honour, we are unaware of any special observance or holiday for atheists."

The judge said, "The calendar says April 1st is April Fools Day. Psalm 14:1 states,

"The fool says in his heart, there is no God.

" Thus, it is the opinion of this court, that, if your client says there is no God, then he is a fool. Therefore, April 1st is his day. Court is adjourned."

You got to love a Judge that knows his scripture!

An Arab enters a taxi. Once he is seated he asks the cab driver to turn off the radio because he must not hear music as decreed by his religion and, in the time of the prophet, there was no music, especially Western music which is music of the infidel's and certainly no radio ....So the cab driver politely switches off the radio, stops the cab and opens the back door. The Arab asks him:

"What are you doing man?"

The cabby answers: "In the time of the prophet there were no taxis. So get out and wait for a camel."

A teacher fell asleep in class and a little naughty boy walked up to him,

Little boy: "teacher are you sleeping in class?"

Teacher: "No I am not sleeping in class."

Little boy: "What were you doing sir?"

Teacher: "I was talking to God."

The next day the naughty boy fell asleep in class and the same teacher walks up to him.

Teacher: "young man, you are sleeping in my class."

Little boy: "No, not me sir, I am not sleeping."

Angry teacher: "What were you doing?"

Little boy: "I was talking to God."

Angry teacher: "What did he say?"

Little boy: "God said he never spoke to you yesterday."

Two engineering students meet on campus one day. The first engineer calls out to the other,

"Hey, Nice bike! Where did you get it?"

"Well," replies the other, "I was walking to class the other day when this pretty, young co-ed rides up on this bike. She jumps off, takes off all of her clothes, and says:

"You can have ANYTHING you want!!"

"Good choice," says the first, "her clothes wouldn't have fit you anyway."

Three pastors in a certain denomination - an American, a Chinese and a Jamaican - were having some difficulty making a decision regarding their Sunday church offering; specifically, which portion they should keep as salary, and which portion should go to the Lord. The American said,

"Whenever I collect the offering and the service is through, I put the money in a box, go outside, take a stick and draw a line on the floor and throw the money in the air. Whatever falls on the right is for the Lord and whatever falls on the left is mine." The Chinese said,

"I put money in box, I don't draw line - I draw circle! I stand in center, throw box wit money in air - whatever fall on outside is mine and what fall inside is for Lord."

The Jamaican then replied: "Mi naw draw circle, mi naw draw line. All me do is put de money inna one box and fling it inna de air.... whateva de Lawd want, him betta grab it quick, cause what drop on de ground a fo mi!"

A little girl asked her mother,

"How did the human race appear?"
The mother answered,

"God made Adam and Eve and they had children and so was all mankind made."
Two days later the girl asked her father the same question.
The father answered,

"Many years ago there were monkeys from which the human race evolved."
The confused girl returned to her mother and said,

"Mom, how is it possible that you told me the human race was created by God, and Dad said they developed from monkeys?"
The mother answered,

"Well, dear, it is very simple. I told you about my side of the family and your father told you about his."

A boy takes a girl on a date. She orders costly champagne, oysters, lobsters, the most expensive food on the menu. The boy asks:

"Do you eat like this at your mother's place."

The girl replies:

"No. My mother doesn't plan to sleep with me."

Husband comes home from Church, greets his wife, lifts her up and carries her around the house. The wife is so surprised and asks smiling,

"Did the Pastor preach about being romantic"?

Out of breath the husband replies,

"No, he said we must carry our burdens..."

A man is sitting at home on the veranda having drinks with his wife and he says,

"I love you".

She asks,

"Is that you or the beer talking?"

He replies, "It's me... talking to the beer."

"Pastor, my dog is dead. Could there be a service for the poor creature?"

Pastor replied,

"No, we cannot have service for an animal in the church. But there is a new church down the road. Maybe they will do something for the animal".

The man answered"

"Pastor, but do you think they will accept a donation of $250,000 in return for the burial service?"

Pastor exclaimed,

"Sweet Jesus! Why didn't u tell me that dog was a Christian."

A beautiful girl was giving a pedicure to a man who was at the same time also getting a shave at a salon. The man says"

"What about a date later?"

"Am married", she replied.

The man said:

"So?, call your husband and tell him you are going to visit a girlfriend"

She said:

"You should tell him yourself, he is shaving you".

Husband: I have a problem at the office.
Wife: After marriage, you don't say I have a problem, say we have a problem.
Husband: Ok. We are expecting a baby from OUR Secretary!

During one of her daily classes, a teacher trying to teach good manners and asked her students the following question:

"Michael, if you were on a date having dinner with a nice young lady, how would you tell her that you have to go to the bathroom?"

Michael said, "Just a minute I have to go pee."

The teacher responded by saying, "That would be rude and impolite. What about you Sherman, how would you say it?"

Sherman said, "I am sorry, but I really need to go to the bathroom. I'll be right back."

"That's better, but it's still not very nice to say the word bathroom at the dinner table. And you, little Johnny, can you use your brain for once and show us your good manners?"

"I would say: Darling, may I please be excused for a moment?, I have to shake hands with a very dear friend of mine, whom I hope to introduce to you after dinner."

The teacher fainted...

After having dug to a depth of 10 feet last year, British scientists found traces of copper wire dating back 200 years and came to the conclusion that their ancestors already had a telephone network more than 150 years ago.

Not to be outdone by the Brit's, in the weeks that followed, an American archaeologist dug to a depth of 20 feet, and shortly after, a story published in the New York bulletin: "American archaeologists, finding traces of 250-year-old copper wire, have concluded that their ancestors already had an advanced high-tech communications network 50 years earlier than the British".

One week later, the Punch Newspaper, in Ibadan, Nigerian, reported the following:

"After digging as deep as 30 feet in his backyard Lucky Ade, a self-taught archaeologist, reported that he found absolutely nothing. Lucky has therefore concluded that more 250 years ago, Africa had already gone wireless."

A Welsh farmer drove to a neighbours farmhouse and knocked at the door. A boy, about 9, opened the door.

"Is your dad or your mum home?" said the farmer.

"No, they went to town."

"How about your brother, Howard? Is he here?"

"No, he went with Mum and Dad."

The farmer stood there for a few minutes, shifting from one foot to the other, and mumbling to himself.

"I know where all the tools are, if you want to borrow one, or I can give dad a message." said the boy.

"Well," said the farmer uncomfortably, "I really wanted to talk to your Dad. It's about your brother, Howard, getting my daughter Susie pregnant".

The boy thought for a moment...

"You would have to talk to Dad about that. I know he charges £500 for the bull and £50 for the pig, but I don't know how much he charges for Howard."

A noted psychiatrist was a guest at a blonde gathering, and his hostess naturally broached the subject in which the doctor was most at ease.

"Would you mind telling me, doctor," she asked, "how you detect a mental deficiency in somebody who appears completely normal?"

"That's easy," he replied. "You ask them a simple question which everyone should be able to answer with no trouble. If they hesitate, that puts you on the right track."

"What sort of question would you ask, doctor?"

"Well, I might ask him... "Captain Cook made three trips around the world and died during one of them. Which one?"

The blonde thought a moment, then said with a nervous laugh:

"You wouldn't happen to have another example would you?, I must confess I don't know much about history."

One sunny day in Ireland, two men were sitting in a pub, drinking some Guinness, when one turns to the other and says:

"You see that man over there?, He looks just like me!, I think I'm gonna go over there and talk to him."
So, he goes over to the man and taps him on the shoulder.

"Excuse me sir" he starts, "but I noticed you look just like me!"
The second man turns around and says:

"Yeah, I noticed the same thing. Where you from?"
"I'm from Dublin" came the reply.
"Me too! What street do you live on?"
"McCarthy street",
The second man replies, "Me too! What number is it?",
"162" the first man replies.
"Me too! What are your parent's names?"
"Connor and Shannon"
The second man, almost dumbfounded says,

"Mine too! This is unbelievable!"
So, they buy some more Guinness and they're talking some more when the bartenders change shifts. The new bartender comes in and goes up to the other bartender and asks:

"What's new today?"
"Oh nothing much, the Murphy twins are drunk again as usual".

An elderly Italian man went to the local church for confession.

When the priest slid open the panel in the confessional, the man said: "Father ... During World War II a beautiful Jewish woman from our neighbourhood knocked urgently on my door and asked me to hide her from the Nazis. So I hid her in my attic."

The priest replied: "That was a wonderful thing you did, and you have no need to confess that!"

"There is more to tell, Father... she started to repay me with sexual favours. This happened several times a week, and sometimes twice on Sundays."

The priest said, "By doing what you did, you placed the two of you in great danger, but two people under those circumstances can easily succumb to the weakness of the flesh. However, if you are truly sorry for your actions, you are indeed forgiven."

"Thank you, Father. That's a great load off my mind. However, I do have one more question."

"And what is that?" asked the priest.
"When should I tell her the war is over?"

Man: I want a divorce. My wife hasn't spoken to me in six months.
Lawyer: Better think it over. Wives like that are hard to get!

An accused bank robber was tried for his crime and was found guilty.

Just prior to being taken away, he looked the judge in the eye and asked, "Would it be okay if I call you a son of a bitch?"

The judge's face reddened as he bellowed, "It most certainly would not! I would add more time to your sentence."

Nodding, the defendant said, "What if I THOUGHT it?, Would that be okay?"

Although annoyed, the judge restrained himself and calmly replied, "Yes, I suppose that would be okay. Obviously, I have no control over your thoughts."

Smirking, the defendant said, "In that case, Judge, I think you're a son of a bitch!"

Catholic men and a Catholic woman were having coffee in St. Peters Square , Rome .

The first Catholic man tells his friends,

"My son is a priest, when he walks into a room, everyone calls him Father".

The second Catholic man chirps,

"My son is a Bishop. When he walks into a room people call him "Your Grace"."

The third Catholic gent says,

"My son is a Cardinal. When he enters a room everyone bows their head and says "Your Eminence"."

The fourth Catholic man says very proudly,

"My son is the Pope. When he walks into a room people call him "Your Holiness"."

Since the lone Catholic woman was sipping her coffee in silence, the four men give her a subtle, "Well...?"

She proudly replies, "I have a daughter,

Slim,

Tall,

38D breast,

24" waist and

34" hips.

When she walks into a room, people say, "My God!"

During the wedding rehearsal, the groom approached the pastor with an unusual offer:

"Look, I'll give you $100 if you'll change the wedding vows. When you get to the part where I'm supposed to promise to "love, honor and obey' and "be faithful to her forever," I'd appreciate it if you'd just leave that out.' He passed the minister a $100 bill and walked away satisfied.

On the day of the wedding, when it came time for the groom's vows, the pastor looked the young man in the eye and said: "Will you promise to prostrate yourself before her, obey her every command and wish, serve her breakfast in bed every morning of your life, and swear eternally before God and your lovely wife that you will not ever even look at another woman, as long as you both shall live?"

The groom gulped and looked around, and said in a tiny voice,

"Yes," then leaned toward the pastor and hissed: "I thought we had a deal."

The pastor put a $100 bill into the groom's hand and whispered: "She made me a better offer."

A young lady, goes to her local pet store in search of an exotic pet. As she looks about the store, she notices a box full of live frogs. The sign says:

"Sex Frogs! Only $20 each!
Money Back Guarantee!
Comes with complete instructions."

The girl excitedly looks around to see if anybody's watching her. She whispers softly to the man behind the counter,"I'll take one."

The man packages the frog and says, "Just follow the instructions." The girl nods, grabs the box, and is quickly on her way home. As soon as she closes the door to her apartment, she reads the instructions and reads them very carefully. She does exactly what is specified:

1. Take a shower.
2. Splash on some nice perfume.
3. Slip into a very sexy nightie.
4. Crawl into bed and place the frog down beside you and allow the frog to follow it's training.

She then quickly gets into bed with the frog and, to her surprise, nothing happens!

The girl is very disappointed and quite upset at this point. She rereads the instructions and notices at the bottom of the paper it says, "If you have a problems or questions, please call the pet store."

So, the lady calls the pet store. The man says, "I'll be right over." Within minutes, the man is ringing her doorbell.

The lady welcomes him in and says, "See, I've done everything according to the instructions. The damn thing just sit there."

The man, looking very concerned, picks up the frog, stares directly at the frog and says, "Listen to me! I'm only going to show you how to do this one more time...."

A Newfie went hunting one day in Ontario and bagged three ducks. He put them in the bed of his pickup truck and was about to drive home when he was confronted by an ornery game warden who didn't like Newfies.

The game warden ordered the Newfie to show his hunting license, and the Newfie pulled out a valid Ontario hunting license.

The game warden looked at the license, then reached over and picked up one of the ducks, sniffed its ass, and said, "This duck ain't from Ontario. This is a Quebec duck. You got a Quebec huntin' license, boy?" The Newfie reached into his wallet and produced a Quebec hunting license.

The game warden looked at it, then reached over and grabbed the second duck, sniffed its ass, and said, "This ain't no Quebec duck. This duck's from Manitoba . You got a Manitoba license?" The Newfie reached into wallet and produced a Manitoba hunting license.

The warden then reached over and picked up the third duck, sniffed its ass, and said,

"This ain't no Manitoba duck. This here duck's from Nova Scotia . You got a Nova Scotia huntin' license?" Again the Newfie reached into his wallet and brought out a Nova Scotia hunting license.

The game warden was extremely frustrated at this point, and he yelled at the Newfie,

"Just where the hell are you from?"

The Newfie turned around, bent over, dropped his pants, and said,

"You tell me, you're the expert."

Defense Attorney: Will you please state your age?

Little Old Lady: I am 86 years old.

Defense Attorney: Will you tell us, in your own words, what happened the night of April 1st?

Little Old Lady: There I was, sitting there in my swing on my front porch on a warm spring evening, when a young man comes creeping up on the porch and sat down beside me.

Defense Attorney: Did you know him?

Little Old Lady: No, but he sure was friendly.

Defense Attorney: What happened after he sat down?

Little Old Lady: He started to rub my thigh.

Defense Attorney: Did you stop him?

Little Old Lady: No, I didn't stop him.

Defense Attorney: Why not?

Little Old Lady: It felt good. Nobody had done that since my Albert died some 30 years ago.

Defense Attorney: What happened next?

Little Old Lady: He began to rub my breasts.

Defense Attorney: Did you stop him then?

Little Old Lady: No, I did not stop him.

Defense Attorney: Why not?

Little Old Lady: His rubbing made me feel all alive and excited. I haven't felt that good in years!

Defense Attorney: What happened next?

Little Old Lady: Well, by then, I was feeling so "spicy" that I just laid down and told him "Take me, young man. Take me now!"

Defense Attorney: Did he take you?

Little Old Lady: Hell, no! He just yelled, "April Fool!" And that's when I shot him, the little bastard.

A man was sitting outside the house he was about to be evicted from, he'd divorced his wife, lost his children & job.

He picks up the empty bottle of beer near him, smashes it into the wall as he shouts; "You're the reason I don't have a wife"

To the 2nd bottle he says "You're the reason I lost my children & job" then smashes it!

He sees the 3rd bottle is sealed & still full of beer.

He puts it aside & says to it "Stand aside my friend; I know you were not involved"

One summer day a man came home early from work and was greeted by his wife dressed in very sexy lingerie and heels.

"Tie me up," she purred, "and you can do anything you want."

So, he tied her up and went golfing.

Phone conversation:

WIFE: Where on earth are you?

HUSBAND: Honey, u remember that Jewelery shop where you saw the diamond necklace and you totally fell in love with it. The wife relaxed with a smile.

WIFE: Yes, the king of my heart I remember.

HUSBAND: And you remember I didn't have money to buy it for you at that time & I told you "honey, that necklace will be yours one day" The wife is totally relaxed with a big smile now and even blushing.

WIFE: Yes I remember my love.

HUSBAND: Good! I am in a bar next to that shop!!

A boss was complaining in a staff meeting the other day that he wasn't getting any respect. Later that morning he went to a local sign shop and bought a small sign that read, "I'm the Boss". He then taped it to his office door.

Later that day when he returned from lunch, he found that someone had taped a note to the sign that said, "Your wife called, she wants her sign back!"

Typical macho man married a typical good-looking lady and after the wedding, he laid down the following rules:

"I'll be home when I want, if I want and at what time I want-and I don't expect any hassle from you. I expect a great dinner to be on the table unless I tell you that I won't be home for dinner. I'll go hunting, fishing, boozing and card-playing when I want with my old buddies and don't you give me a hard time about it. Those are my rules. Any comments?"

His new bride said, "No, that's fine with me. Just understand that there will be sex here at seven o'clock every night... whether you're here or not."

A lady was walking past a pet store when a parrot said,

"Hey, lady! You're really ugly!" The lady was furious and continued on her way. On the way home, she passed by the pet store again and the parrot once more said:

"Hey, lady! You're really ugly!" She was incredibly ticked now, so she went into the store and said that she would sue the store and kill the bird. The store manager apologized profusely and promised he would make sure the parrot didn't say it again.

The next day, she deliberately passed by the store to test the parrot.
"Hey, lady!" it said.

"Yes?"
"You know."

A Mafia Godfather, accompanied by his attorney, walks into a room to meet with his former accountant. The Godfather asks the accountant:

"Where is the 3 million bucks you embezzled from me?"

The accountant does not answer. The Godfather asks again, "Where is the 3 million bucks you embezzled from me?"

The attorney interrupts, "Sir, the man is a deaf mute and cannot understand you, but I can interpret for you."

The Godfather says, "Well ask him where my damn money is!" The attorney, using sign language, asks the accountant where the 3 million dollars is.

The accountant signs back, "I don't know what you are talking about."

The attorney interprets to the Godfather, "He doesn't know what you are talking about." The Godfather pulls out a 9 millimeter pistol, puts it to the temple of the accountant, cocks the trigger and says,

"Ask him again where my damn money is!"

The attorney signs to the accountant, "He wants to know where it is!"

The accountant signs back, "OK! OK! OK! The money is hidden in a brown suitcase behind the shed in my backyard!"

The Godfather says, "Well....what did he say?"

The attorney interprets to the Godfather, "He says...go to hell...that you don't have the guts to pull the trigger."

One day, Pete complained to his friend, "My elbow really hurts. I guess I should see a doctor."

His friend said, "Don't do that. There's a computer at the drug store that can diagnose anything quicker and cheaper than a doctor. Simply put in a sample of your urine, and the computer will diagnose your problem and tell you what you can do about and it will only costs you $10.00."

Pete figured he had nothing to lose, so he filled a jar with a urine sample and went to the drug store. Finding the computer, he poured in the sample and deposited the $10.00.

The computer started making some noise and various lights started flashing. After a brief pause, out popped a small slip of paper which read:

1. You have tennis elbow.

2. Soak your arm in warm water, avoid heavy labor.

3. It will be better in two weeks.

That evening while thinking how amazing this new technology was and how it would change medical science forever, he began to wonder if this computer could be fooled.

He decided to give it a try. He mixed together some tap water, a stool sample from his dog, and urine samples from his wife and daughter. To top it off, he masturbated into the concoction.

He went back to the drug store, located the computer, poured in the sample and deposited the $10.00. The machine again made the usual noises, flashed it's alights, and printed out the following analysis:

1. Your tap water is too hard.

2. Get a water softener.

3. Your dog has ringworm.

4. Bathe him with anti-fungal shampoo.

5. Your daughter is using cocaine.

6. Put her in a rehabilitation clinic.

7. Your wife is pregnant ... twin girls. They aren't yours. Get a lawyer.

8. And if you don't stop masturbating, your elbow will never get better

---

The scene is the darkest jungle in Africa. Two tigers are stalking through the jungle when the one in the rear suddenly reaches out with his tongue and licks the butt of the one in front. The lead tiger turns and says, "Hey, cut it out, alright." The other tiger says sorry and they continue on their way.

After about five minutes the rear tiger suddenly repeats his action. The front tiger turns angrily and says," I said don't do that again!" The rear tiger says "sorry" again and they continue. After about another five minutes, the rear tiger repeats his action. The front tiger turns and says, "What is it with you, anyway? I said to stop." The rear tiger says, "I really am sorry but I just ate a lawyer and I'm just trying to get the taste out of my mouth."

One day a lawyer was riding in his limousine when he saw a guy eating grass. He told the driver to stop. He got out and asked him, "Why are you eating grass?"

The man replied, "I'm so poor, I can't afford anything thing to eat."

So the layer said, "Poor guy, come back to my house."

The guys says, "But I have a wife and three kids." The lawyer told him to bring them along.

When they were all in the car, the poor man said, "Thanks for taking us back to your house, it is so kind of you."

The lawyer replied, "You're going to love it there... the grass is a foot tall!"

Q: Doctor, how many autopsies have you performed on dead people?
A: All my autopsies are performed on dead people.
Q: Do you recall the time that you examined the body?
A: The autopsy started around 8:30 p.m.
Q: And Mr. Dennington was dead at the time?

A: No, he was sitting on the table wondering why I was doing an autopsy.

There is a truck driver who whenever he sees a lawyer walking down the street, he always swerves to hit him. One day he sees a priest on the side of the road looking for a ride and so the truck driver picks him up.

While they were driving, the driver sees a lawyer, and swerves to hit him. But then he remembered he had a priest in the truck, so he swerved back on the road, but he heard a loud "thump" anyway.

So the driver turns to the priest and says "Please forgive me," and the priest said, "You didn't hit the lawyer, but that's OK, I got him with the door."

A Lawyer runs a stop sign and gets pulled over by a Sheriff,s Deputy. He thinks that he is smarter than the Deputy because he is sure that he has a better education. He decides to prove this to himself and have some fun at the deputy,s expense.

Deputy says, "License and registration, please."
Lawyer says, "What for?"

Deputy says, "You didn't come to a complete stop at the stop sign "

Lawyer says, "I slowed down, and no one was coming."

Deputy says, "You still didn't come to a complete stop. License and registration, please."

Lawyer says, "What's the difference?"

Deputy says, "The difference is, you have to come to a complete stop, that's the law. License and registration, please!"

Lawyer says, "If you can show me the legal difference between "SLOW DOWN" and "STOP", I'll give you my license and registration and you give me the ticket, if not you let me go and no ticket."

Deputy says, "Exit your vehicle, sir."

At this point, the Deputy takes out his nightstick and starts beating the ever-loving crap out of the Lawyer and says: "DO YOU WANT ME TO STOP OR JUST SLOW DOWN?

A Woman was out golfing one day when she hit the ball into the woods.

She went into the woods to look for it and found a frog in a trap.

The frog said to her, "If you release me from this trap, I will grant you three wishes."

The woman freed the frog, and the frog said, "Thank you, but I failed to mention that there was a condition to your wishes. Whatever you wish for, your husband will get times ten!"

The woman said, "That's okay."

For her first wish, she wanted to be the most beautiful woman in the world.

The frog warned her, "You do realize that this wish will also make your husband the most handsome man in the world, an Adonis whom women will flock to".

The woman replied, "That's okay, because I will be the most beautiful woman and he will have eyes only for me."

So, KAZAM-she's the most beautiful woman in the world!

For her second wish, she wanted to be the richest woman in the world.

The frog said, "That will make your husband the richest man in the world. And he will be ten times richer than you."

The woman said, "That's okay, because what's mine is his and what's his is mine."

So, KAZAM-she's the richest woman in the world!

The frog then inquired about her third wish, and she answered, "I'd like a mild heart attack."

A physicist, biologist and a chemist were going to the ocean for the first time.

The physicist saw the ocean and was fascinated by the waves. He said he wanted to do some research on the fluid dynamics of the waves and walked into the ocean. Obviously he was drowned and never returned.

The biologist said he wanted to do research on the flora and fauna inside the ocean and walked inside the ocean. He too, never returned.

The chemist waited for a long time and afterwards, wrote the observation, "The physicist and the biologist are soluble in ocean water".

A MAN WALKS INTO A BAR and sits down next to a lady and a dog.

The man asks, "Does your dog bite?"
The lady answers, "Never!"

The man reaches out to pat the dog and the dog bites him. The man says, "I thought you said your dog doesn't bite!"

The woman replies, "He doesn't. This isn't my dog."

A guy walks into a bar and says to bartender give four shots of your best scotch right now. The bartender pours them up and sets them in front of the man. The man slams back all four of them one right after the other.

Bartender says: "man you must be in a hurry?",
The man says: "you would be too if you had only twenty-five cents."

A man went to the Police Station wishing to speak with the burglar who had broken into his house the night before.

"You'll get your chance in court." said the Desk Sergeant.
"No, no, no!" said the man. "I want to know how he got into the house without waking my wife. I've been trying to do that for years!"

An Russian tourist in New-York found himself needing to get rid of a large supply of garbage from his recent stay at an apartment. After a long search, he just couldn't find any place to discard of it. So, he just went down one of the side streets to dump it there.

Yet, he was stopped by a police officer, who said,
"Hey you, what are you doing?"
"I have to throw this away," replied the tourist.

"You can't throw it away here. Look, follow me," the policeman offered.

The police officer led him to a beautiful garden with lots of grass, pretty flowers, and manicured hedges.

"Here," said the cop, "dump all the garbage you want."

The russian shrugs, opens up the large bags of garbage, and dumps them right on the flowers.

"Thanks for giving me a place to dump this stuff. This is very nice of you. Is this U.S.A courtesy?" asked the tourist.

"No. This is the Russian Embassy."

A visitor from Holland was chatting with his American friend and was jokingly explaining about the red, white and blue in the Netherlands flag.

"Our flag symbolizes our taxes," he said. "We get red when we talk about them, white when we get our tax bill, and blue after we pay them."

"That's the same with us." the American said, "only we see stars, too."

A US Border Patrol Agent catches an illegal alien in the bushes right by the border fence, he pulls him out and says:

"Sorry, you know the law, you've got to go back across the border right now."

The mexican man pleads with them, "No, noooo Senior, I must stay in de USA! Pleeeze!"

The Border Patrol Agent thinks to himself, I'm going to make it hard for him and says: "Ok, I'll let you stay if you can use 3 english words in a sentence"

The Mexican man of course agrees.

The Border Patrol Agent tells him, "The 3 words are: Green, Pink and Yellow. Now use them in 1 sentence."

The Mexican man thinks really hard for about 2 minutes, then says, "Hmmm, Ok. The phone, it went Green, Green, Green, I Pink it up and sez Yellow?"

Three men are traveling in the Amazon, a German, an American, and a Mexican, and they get captured by some Amazons. The head of the tribe says to the German,

"What do you want on your back for your whipping?",

The German responds, "I will take oil!".

So they put oil on his back, and a large Amazon whips him ten times. When he is finished the German has these huge welts on his back, and he can hardly move.

The Amazons haul the German away, and say to the Mexican, "What do you want on your back?"

"I will take nothing!" says the Mexican, and he stands there straight and takes his ten lashings without a single flinch.

"What will you take on your back?" the Amazons ask the American.

He responds, "I'll take the Mexican."

A father passing by his teenage daughter's bedroom was astonished to see the bed was nicely made and everything was neat and tidy.

Then he saw an envelope propped up prominently on the centre of the pillow. It was addressed "Dad". With the worst premonition, he opened the envelope and read the letter with trembling hands:

"Dear Dad,

It is with great regret and sorrow that I'm writing you, but I'm leaving home. I had to elope with my new boyfriend Randy because I wanted to avoid a scene with Mom and you. I've been finding real passion with Randy and he is so nice to me. I know when you meet him you'll like him too - even with all his piercing, tattoos, and motorcycle clothes. But it's not only the passion Dad, I'm pregnant and Randy said that he wants me to have the kid and that we can be very happy together.

Even though Randy is much older than me (anyway, 42 isn't so old these days is it?), and has no money, really these things shouldn't stand in the way of our relationship, don't you agree? Randy has a great CD collection; he already owns a trailer in the woods and has a stack of firewood for the whole winter. It's true he has other girlfriends as well but I know he'll be faithful to me in his own way. He wants to have many more children with me and that's now one of my dreams too. Randy taught me that marijuana doesn't really hurt anyone and he'll be growing it for us and we'll trade it with our friends for all the cocaine and ecstasy we want. In the meantime, we'll pray that science will find a cure for AIDS so Randy can get better; he sure deserves it!!

Don't worry Dad, I'm 15 years old now and I know how to take care of myself. Someday I'm sure we'll be back to visit so you can get to know your grandchildren.

Your loving daughter,

Rosie."

At the bottom of the page were the letters " PTO".

Hands still trembling, her father turned the sheet, and read:

PS:

Dad, none of the above is true. I'm over at the neighbors house. I just wanted to remind you that there are worse things in life than my report card that's in my desk center drawer. Please sign it and call when it is safe for me to come home.

I love you!

Your loving daughter,

Rosie

An Nigerian man had no child, no money, no home and a blind mother.

He prayed to God. God was happy with his prayers and told him to make only ONE wish which will be granted!

Nigerian man: I want my mother to see my wife putting Diamond bangles on my child's hands in our new mansion which has a sea view!

God: Damn! I still have a lot to learn from these Nigerians!

A guy stood over his tee shot for what seemed an eternity; looking up, looking down, measuring the distance, figuring the wind direction and speed. Driving his partner nuts. Finally his exasperated partner says, "What's taking so long? Hit the blasted ball!"

The guy answers, "My wife is up there watching me from the clubhouse. I want to make this a perfect shot."

"Forget it, man! You don't stand a chance of hitting her from here!"

"The thrill is gone from my marriage," Bill told his friend Doug.

Doug suggests, "Why not add some intrigue to your life and have an affair?"

"But what if my wife finds out?" asks Bill.

"Heck, this is a new age we live in, Bill. Go ahead and tell her about it!" said Doug.

So Bill went home and said, "Dear, I think an affair will bring us closer together."

"Forget it," said his wife. "I've tried that? it didn't work."

A couple had been married for 25 years and was celebrating the husband's 60th birthday.

During the party, a fairy appeared and said that because they had been such a loving couple all those years, she would give them one wish each.

The wife said, "We've been so poor all these years, and I've never gotten to see the world. I wish we could travel all over the world." The fairy waved her wand and POOF! She had the tickets in her hand.

Next, it was the husband's turn. He paused for a moment, and then said, "Well, I'd like to be married to a woman 30 years younger than me."

The fairy waved her wand and POOF! He was suddenly 90 years old!

A few moments after the daughter announced her engagement, her Father asked, "Does this fellow have any money ?"

The daughter shook her head sadly.

"Oh Daddy! You men are all alike." sighing deeply, she replied, "That's exactly what he asked me about you."

A man was walking in the street when he heard a voice.

"Stop! Stand still! If you take one more step, a brick will fall down on your head and kill you." The man stopped and a big brick fell right in front of him. The man was astonished.

He went on, and after a while he was going to cross the road. Once again the voice shouted:

"Stop! Stand still! If you take one more step a car will run over you and you will die.

The man did as he was instructed, just as a car came careening around the corner, barely missing him.

"Where are you?" the man asked. "Who are you?"

"I am your guardian angel," the voice answered.

"Oh yeah?" the man asked. "And where the hell were you when I got married?"

A husband crawls back home drunk on night. Next day he wakes up with a hangover and sees that the whole house is clean and his shirts are laundered and there is a breakfast already prepared.

So he asks his son:

"Hey Billy, what is up, why is your mother so nice to me considering my condition last night?"

Billy answers: "Well, yesterday when she was pulling your pants off you were yelling: "Get away from be, bitch! I'm married!""

A husband and wife were sitting watching a TV program about psychology when he turned to his wife and said,

"Honey, I bet you can't tell me something that will make me happy and sad at the same time."

She said, "You have a bigger d**k than all of your friends."

One man enters in an ambulant and says to the doctor:
- Help me, please. I have a knife in my back.

The doctor, looking his watch says:
- Now is 2:20 PM, and I work till 2:00, so as you can imagine I've finished for today, and I can't help you. Be so kind and come tomorrow morning, at 8:00.

- But tomorrow morning I will be dead. You must help me now.

The doctor, angrily says: "I explained to you gently that I've finished my shift for today, and that I can't do nothing for you. You must pass here tomorrow.

- But, until tomorrow I will lose all my blood, and I will be dead. Don't you see that I have a knife in the back.

The doctor, already very angry and irritate extracts the knife from the back, and put it in the patients eye.

- Now you can go to ophthalmologist, he works till 3 PM.

Little Mario comes back from the school crying.
- Mum, everybody in the school calls me "mafioso".
- Don't worry, my son. Tomorrow I will go to see the principal.
- Thank you mum. Please make it look like an accident.

A man walks by the sea and suddenly hears someone yelling:
- Help, help! I'm drowning, I don't know how to swim!
He turns around, notices a man drowning, and asks:
- Parla Italiano?
The drowning man says:
- Si, si! Parlo Italiano! Aiuto, per favore!
- You idiot! It would have been better for you to learn how to swim than to learn Italian.

A little boy asked his mother:
- Mummy, why are you white and I am black?
- Don't even ask me that, when I remember that party..., you are lucky that you don't bark.

Submarines are safer than airplanes. Proof in the fact is there are more airplanes in the water than submarines in the air!

As we stood in formation at the Pensacola Naval Air Station, our Flight Instructor said, "All right! All you dummies fall out."
As the rest of the squad wandered away, I remained at attention.
The instructor walked over until he was eye-to-eye with me, and then just raised a single eyebrow. I smiled and said, "Sure was a lot of 'em, huh sir?"

A soldier serving in Hong Kong was annoyed and upset when his girl wrote breaking off their engagement and asking for her photograph back.

He went out and collected from his friends all the unwanted photographs of women that he could find, bundled them all together and sent them back with a note saying,

"I regret to inform you that I cannot remember which one is you - please keep your photo and return the others."

There were two Indians and a Polish fellow walking along together in the desert, when, all of a sudden, one of the Indians took off and ran up a hill to the mouth of a cave.

He stopped and hollered into the cave: "Woooooo! Woooooo! Woooooo!" and then listened very closely until he heard the answer:"Woooooo! Woooooo! Woooooo!" He then tore off his clothes and ran in to the cave. The Polish fellow was puzzled and asked the other Indian what that was all about, was that Indian goofy or something.

"No", said the other Indian. "It is mating time for us Indians and when you see a cave and holler, "Woooooo! Woooooo! Woooooo!", and get an answer back, that means that she is in there waiting for you.

Well, just about that time, the other Indian saw another cave. He took off and ran up to the cave, then stopped and hollered, "Woooooo! Woooooo! Woooooo!" When he heard the return, "Woooooo! Woooooo! Woooooo!", off came the clothes and into the cave he goes.

The Polack started running around the desert looking for a cave to find these women that the Indians had talked about. All of a sudden, he looked up and saw this great big cave.

As he looked in amazement, he was thinking, "Man! Look at the size of that cave! It's bigger than the ones that those Indians found. There must really be something really great in this cave!"

Well... he took-off up the hill at a superfast speed. He got in front of the cave and hollered, "Wooooo! Woooooo! Woooooo!" He was just tickled all over when he heard the answering call of, "WOOOOOOOOOO! WOOOOOOOOOO!! WOOOOOOOOOO!!! Off came his clothes and, with a big smile on his face, he raced into the cave.

The next day in the newspaper the headlines read, Naked Polack Run Over By Freight Train!!

An evil Atheist explorer in the deepest Amazon suddenly finds himself surrounded by a bloodthirsty group of natives. Upon surveying the situation, he says quietly to himself: "Oh God, I'm screwed!!!!!."

There is a ray of light from heaven and a voice booms out:

"No, you are NOT screwed. Pick up that stone at your feet and bash in the head of the chief standing in front of you

So the explorer picks up the stone and proceeds to bash the living heck out of the chief.

As he stands above the lifeless body, breathing heavily and surrounded by 100 natives with a look of shock on their faces, Gods voice booms out again: "Okay ..... NOW you're screwed."

A new man is brought into Prison Cell 102. Already there is a long-time resident who looks 100 years old. The new man looks at the old-timer inquiringly. The old-timer says,

"Look at me. I'm old and worn out. You'd never believe that I used to live the life of Riley. I wintered on the Riviera, had a boat, four fine cars, the most beautiful women, and I ate in all the best restaurants of France."

The new man asked, "What happened?"

"One day Riley reported his credit cards missing!"

Driving to work, a gentleman had to swerve to avoid a box that fell out of a truck in front of him. Seconds later, a policeman pulled him over for reckless driving. Fortunately, another officer had seen the carton in the road. The policemen stopped traffic and recovered the box. It was found to contain large upholstery tacks.

"I'm sorry sir," the first trooper told the driver, "but I am still going to have to write you a ticket."

"Why?" the driver asked.

The trooper replied, "Tacks evasion."

Bill and Hillary were going down a back road and stopped at a gas station. As the worker was filling up their car, he said to Hillary:

"I went to high school with you". She recognized him and agreed with him. Later as they were driving down the road Bill said:

"If you had married him you wouldn't be married to the President".

Hillary said "Oh yes I would-he would be President."

Woman: Doctor, Doctor my son has swallowed my pen, what should I do?
Doctor: Use a pencil till I get there!

2 sharks swimming around survivors of a sunken ship.

"Follow me son" the father said, "First we swim around them a few times with just the tip of our fins showing & then a few times with all of our fins showing before we eat everybody"

Why? Asked the shark son.

"Because they taste better without the shit inside!" replied father shark!

Heard on a public transportation vehicle in Orlando.

"When you exit the bus, please be sure to lower your head and watch your step."

"If you miss your step and hit your head, please lower your voice and watch your language. Thank you."

A man was driving down a quiet country lane when out into the road strayed a rooster. Whack! The rooster disappeared under the car. A cloud of feathers. Shaken, the man pulled over at the farmhouse, rang the doorbell. A farmer appeared. The man, somewhat nervously said,

"I think I killed your rooster, please allow me to replace him."

"Suit yourself," the farmer replied, "you can go join the other chickens that are around the back."

A motorist was mailed a picture of his car speeding through an automated radar. A $40 speeding ticket was included. Being cute, he sent the police department a picture of $40. The police responded with another mailed photo of handcuffs.

In a very small alley two trucks driving in opposite directions meet. As the drivers are equally stubborn, neither of them wants to reverse. They angrily look one at the other. Finally, one of them picks up a newspaper and starts reading. The other one politely asks,

"When you've finished the paper, will you please bring it over, and let me read it?"

A car was involved in an accident in a street. As expected a large crowd gathered. A newspaper reporter, anxious to get his story could not get near the car. Being a clever sort, he started shouting loudly,

"Let me through! Let me through! I am the son of the victim."

The crowd made way for him. Lying in front of the car was a donkey.

As he lay on his deathbed, the man confided to his wife,

"I cannot die without telling you the truth. I cheated on you throughout our whole marriage. All those nights when I told you I was working late, I was with other women. And not just one woman either, but I've slept with dozens of them."

His wife looked at him calmly and said, "Why do you think I gave you the poison?"

On a rural road a state trooper pulled a farmer over and said:

"Sir, do you realize your wife fell out of the car several miles back?"

To which the farmer replied: "Thank God, I thought I had gone deaf!"

NASA was interviewing professionals to be sent to Mars. Only one could go and couldn't return to Earth.

The first applicant, an engineer, was asked how much he wanted to be paid for going. "A million dollars," he answered, "because I want to donate it to M.I.T."

The next applicant, a doctor, was asked the same question. He asked for $2 million. "I want to give a million to my family," he explained, "and leave the other million for the advancement of medical research."

The last applicant was a lawyer. When asked how much money he wanted, he whispered in the interviewer's ear, "Three million dollars."

"Why so much more than the others?" asked the interviewer.

The lawyer replied, "If you give me $3 million, I'll give you $1 million, I'll keep $1 million, and we'll send the engineer to Mars."

"How can I ever thank you?" gushed a woman to Clarence Darrow, after he had solved her legal troubles.

"My dear woman," Darrow replied, "ever since the Phoenicians invented money there has been only one answer to that question."

A man in a hospital bed called for his doctor & asked,

"Give it to me straight. How long have I got?" The physician replied that he doubted the man would survive the night.

The man then said, "Call for my lawyer." When the lawyer arrived, the man asked his physician to stand on one side of the bed & the lawyer on the other. The man then laid back & closed his eyes. When asked what he had in mind, he replied:

"Jesus died with a thief on either side. I just thought I'd check out the same way."

A man is strolling past the mental hospital and suddenly remembers an important meeting. Unfortunately, his watch has stopped, and he cannot tell if he is late or not. Then, he notices a patient similarly strolling about within the hospital fence.

Calling out to the patient, the man says, "Pardon me, sir, but do you have the time?"

The patient calls back, "One moment!" and throws himself upon the ground, pulling out a short stick as he does. He pushes the stick into the ground, and, pulling out a carpenter's level, assures himself that the stick is vertical.

With a compass, the patient locates north and with a steel ruler, measures the precise length of the shadow cast by the stick.

Withdrawing a slide rule from his pocket, the patient calculates rapidly, then swiftly packs up all his tools and turns back to the pedestrian, saying, "It is now precisely 3:29 pm, provided today is August 16th, which I believe it is."

The man can't help but be impressed by this demonstration, and sets his watch accordingly.

Before he leaves, he says to the patient, "That was really quite remarkable, but tell me, what do you do on a cloudy day, or at night, when the stick casts no shadow?"

The patient holds up his wrist and says, "I suppose I'd just look at my watch."

After hearing that one of the patients in a mental hospital had saved another from a suicide attempt by pulling him out of a bathtub, the hospital director reviewed the rescuers file and called him into his office.

"Mr. Haroldson, your records and your heroic behavior indicate that you're ready to go home. I'm only sorry that the man you saved later killed himself with a rope around the neck."

"Oh, he didn't kill himself," Mr. Haroldson replied. "I hung him up to dry."

A man runs to the doctor and says, "Doctor, you've got to help me. My wife thinks she's a chicken!"

The doctor asks, "How long has she had this condition?"

"Two years," says the man.

"Then why did it take you so long to come and see me?" asked the shrink.

The man shrugs his shoulders and replies, "We needed the eggs."

A lady goes to deposit $1000 in a bank, the teller says, sorry madam these notes are counterfeit. "Oh my God!!" exclaimed the lady, "I have been raped !".

Little Amy confided to her uncle, "When I grow up, I'm going to marry the boy next door."

"Why is that?"
"Cause I'm not allowed to cross the road."

An airliner was having engine trouble, and the pilot instructed the cabin crew to have the passengers take their seats and get prepared for an emergency landing.

A few minutes later, the pilot asked the flight attendants if everyone was buckled in and ready.

"All set back here, Captain," came the reply, "except the lawyers are still going around passing out business cards."

Taxiing down the tarmac, the jetliner abruptly stopped, turned around and returned to the gate. After an hour-long wait, it finally took off.

A concerned passenger asked the flight attendant, "What was the problem?"

"The pilot was bothered by a noise he heard in the engine," explained the Flight Attendant, "and it took us a while to find a new pilot."

As migration approached, two elderly vultures doubted they could make the trip south, so they decided to go by airplane. When they checked their baggage, the attendant noticed that they were carrying two dead raccoons.

"Do you wish to check the raccoons through as luggage?" she asked.

"No, thanks," replied the vultures. "They're carrion."

The psychology instructor had just finished a lecture on mental health and was giving an oral test.

Speaking specifically about manic depression, she asked,

"How would you diagnose a patient who walks back and forth screaming at the top of his lungs one minute, then sits in a chair weeping uncontrollably the next?"

A young man in the rear raised his hand and answered, "A basketball coach?"

An Army brat was boasting about his father to a Navy brat.

"My dad is an engineer. He can do everything. Do you know the Alps?"

"Yes," said the Navy brat.

"My dad has built them."

Then the naval kid spoke: "And do you know the Dead Sea?"

"Yes."

"It's my dad who's killed it!"

A new York Divorce Lawyer died and arrived at the pearly gates. Saint Peter asks him:

"What have you done to merit entrance into Heaven?"

The Lawyer thought a moment, then said,

"A week ago, I gave a quarter to a homeless person on the street."

Saint Peter asked Gabriel to check this out in the record, and after a moment Gabriel affirmed that this was true. Saint Peter said,

"Well, that's fine, but it's not really quite enough to get you into Heaven." The Lawyer said,

"Wait, Wait! There's more! Three years ago I also gave a homeless person a quarter."

Saint Peter nodded to Gabriel, who after a moment nodded back, affirming this, too, had been verified. Saint Peter then whispered to Gabriel,

"Well, what do you suggest we do with this fellow?"

Gabriel gave the Lawyer a sidelong glance, then said to Saint Peter,

"Let's give him back his 50 cents and tell him to go to Hell."

Three men were standing in line to get into heaven one day. Apparently it had been a pretty busy day, though, so Peter had to tell the first one,

"Heaven's getting pretty close to full today, and I've been asked to admit only people who have had particularly horrible deaths. So what's your story?"

So the first man replies:

"Well, for a while I've suspected my wife has been cheating on me, so today I came home early to try to catch her red-handed. As I came into my 25th floor apartment, I could tell something was wrong, but all my searching around didn't reveal where this other guy could have been hiding. Finally, I went out to the balcony, and sure enough, there was this man hanging off the railing, 25 floors above ground! By now I was really mad, so I started beating on him and kicking him, but wouldn't you know it, he wouldn't fall off. So finally I went back into my apartment and got a hammer and starting hammering on his fingers. Of course, he couldn't stand that for long, so he let go and fell, but even after 25 stories, he fell into the bushes, stunned but okay. I couldn't stand it anymore, so I ran into the kitchen, grabbed the fridge and threw it over the edge where it landed on him, killing him instantly. But all the stress and anger got to me, and I had a heart attack and died there on the balcony."

"That sounds like a pretty bad day to me," said Peter, and let the man in.

The second man comes up and Peter explains to him about heaven being full, and again asks for his story.

"It's been a very strange day. You see, I live on the 26th floor of my apartment building, and every morning I do my exercises out on my balcony. Well, this morning I must have slipped or something, because I fell over the edge. But I got lucky, and caught the railing of the balcony on the floor below me. I knew I couldn't hang on for very long, when suddenly this man burst out onto the balcony. I thought for sure I was saved, when he started beating on me and kicking me. I held on the best I could until he ran into the apartment and grabbed a hammer and started pounding on my hands. Finally I just let go, but again I got lucky and fell into the bushes below, stunned but all right. Just when I was thinking I was going to be okay, this refrigerator comes falling out of the sky and crushes me instantly, and now I'm here."

Once again, Peter had to concede that that sounded like a pretty horrible death.

The third man came to the front of the line, and again Peter explained that heaven was full and asked for his story.

"Picture this," says the third man, "I'm hiding inside a refrigerator..."

A small boy is sent to bed by his father...
[5mins later]
"Da-ad...",
"What?",
"I'm thirsty. Can you bring me a drink of water?",
"No. You had your chance. Lights out.",
[5mins later]
"Da-aaaad...",
"WHAT?",
"I'm THIRSTY...Can I have a drink of water??"
"I told you NO! If you ask again I'll have to spank you!!",
[5mins later]
"Daaaa-aaaAAAAD...",
"WHAT??!!",
"When you come in to spank me, can you bring me a drink of water?"

A very successful businessman had a meeting with his new son-in-law.
"I love my daughter, and now I welcome you into the family." said the man. "To show you how much we care for you, I'm making you a 50-50 partner in my business. All you have to do is go to the factory every day and learn the operations."
The son-in-law interrupted, "I hate factories. I can't stand the noise."

"I see," replied the father-in-law. "Well, then you'll work in the office and take charge of some of the operations."

"I hate office work," said the son-on-law. "I can't stand being stuck behind a desk all day."

"Wait a minute," said the father-in-law. "I just make you half-owner of a moneymaking organization, but you don't like factories and won't work in a office. What am I going to do with you?"

"Easy," said the young man. "Buy me out."

Martin had just received his brand new driver license. The family troops out to the driveway, and climbs in the car, where he is going to take them for a ride for the first time. Dad immediately heads for the back seat, directly behind the newly minted driver.

"I'll bet you're back there to get a change of scenery after all those months of sitting in the front passenger seat teaching me how to drive," says the beaming boy to his father.

"Nope," comes dad's reply, "I'm gonna sit here and kick the back of your seat as you drive, just like you've been doing to me all these years."

Made in the USA
San Bernardino, CA
04 January 2018